ON THE WAY TO THE FUNERAL, FUNNY THINGS HAPPEN!

Andrea Oden

ISBN: 979-8-9880086-2-0

On the Way to the Funeral, Funny Things Happen!

Dedication

To the cherished friends and family of Peter Oden, my extraordinary dad, this book is lovingly and laughingly dedicated to you all. It's a testament to the countless moments of awkward hilarity we've endured since his departure, moments he'd surely have laughed at right along with us. May we continue to find humor in the oddities of life, as he so often did. Here's to remembering my dad, not with sorrow, but with the infectious laughter and joy he brought into each of our lives. Dad, we miss you but know you found laughter as you watched the shenanigans that happened on the way to the funeral!

Contents

IN MY FAMILY, THERE'S ALWAYS LAUGHTER

In my family, we are always looking for the jokes, the laughter, the stories that make everything better. In July of 2023 my father passed away. In true Oden form, we had many moments where one of us would turn to the other and say something like:

"Did you see that?"

"Can you believe what he just asked?"

"Are you kidding me?"

"Is it me, or is that crazy?"

As we went through the pain of losing the patriarch of our family, a lot of crazy things happened. As we all talked with friends and other family members, we learned it was not just us, but every family, has funny stories to tell when a black person passes away. It's not that we were insensitive, it's just that the humor is the only thing keeping us from letting our emotions take over.

This collection of stories is all about how people navigate this complicated time in life with humor and love. We have compiled some of the funniest moments for you.

So, this book invites you into the fun, crazy, hilariously inappropriate moments that happen as you plan a funeral. From the people who are dressed just slightly wrong for the service to the person who gets too drunk and causes a scene, this book will show all of us how to laugh in the face of death. It's okay to cry and it's okay to find something funny - we can still celebrate life even as we mourn.

Throughout this book, we'll tell stories of people doing the craziest things from the time a loved one passes away until a week after the funeral services. We have changed the names not only to protect the innocent, but to be able to attend the next family reunion. Some of these stores are about our family, while others are from our friends who kept us laughing as we grieved.

Ready to hear some crazy stories? Here are the funny stories, the crazy, insensitive things that happen on the way to the funeral.

Let's get to it!

Chapter 1

DAY ONE: THE HOSPITAL HOOPLA

Let's kick it off with the day that sets the scene for all the crazy that's about to unfold: the day a loved one dies. Now, you'd think this would be the most somber part, right? But oh, how you'd be mistaken. The hospital room becomes a stage for a comedy of errors, where everyone seems to forget the script. If you've ever sat at the hospital bed of someone as they transition, you know that there are some strange things that happen.

From the doctor who insists on being dramatic when giving out the news, to the nurse who can't help but give a play-by-play of every move she makes, to the family members who out of nowhere start praying. And I don't mean the silent, catholic kind, I mean the loud, Baptist prayers where you find yourself wondering if the prayer will ever end.

In the black culture, church families often visit the hospital. From the pastor to the deacons, this means one thing: Prayer, prayer and more prayer. You think it would be good but it's not. It's the same freakin prayer every time. It's like they are all reading from a prayer book.

Each time a preacher or deacon offers prayer, the family members have to stand and hold hands. It starts something like this:

Most gracious, heavenly father, we come knowing that you are a healer...

Ten minutes in even the most holy of Christians is ready to give a side-eye to the deacon. But you don't want to be disrespectful, so you just stand there and look up for divine intervention.

But what about the people who aren't religious? Don't they get to just sit in peace without someone's hands waving around them mouthing words that don't make any sense? Well, not always. Some preachers, deacons and even some family members feel the need to "bless" everyone as they enter and exit. If you're not ready for it, you'll get a holy water shock.

All this craziness is just the beginning of what's in store when a black person dies.

If it isn't bad enough that the church folks give you long prayers, what about the crazy cousin that missed his calling as a preacher. He calls himself a prophet or some other title that he believes gives him the right to hold the family hostage again in prayer.

In our family, this was Curtis. Curtis screamed, shouted and spoke in tongues for over fifteen straight minutes. To this day we owe the nurse in ICU an Amazon gift card for rescuing us from that prayer.

Nurse Debbie poked her head in the first time and caught my eye. Ten minutes later she came in and caught my fed-up look as well as my brother's pleading eyes, "please... do something."

Nurse Debbie came to the rescue by tapping Cousin Curtis on the shoulder in the middle of his holy ghost antics and told him it was time for her to administer some medication so only the immediate family could be in the room.

Bless you Nurse Debbie!

Uncle Bernie is also there to offer his opinion on what needs to be done and how it needs to be done. Uncle Bernie used to work at hospital. He's been retired for about twenty years, but he knows everything that goes on in hospitals. Was Uncle Bernie a doctor? Maybe a nurse or an orderly? No Uncle Bernie worked in the cafeteria. But that doesn't make him any less knowledgeable about every machine, every drug, and every person in the hospital.

He's always ready to tell you what needs to be done and why it isn't being done correctly. He's quick to point out that the wrong drugs are being given or how they need more staff on the floor. All this while wearing his old hospital scrubs. Why he wears them to the hospital when he's been retired for fifteen years? Your guess is as good as mine.

We mustn't forget about Felicia. While she is indeed a nurse, she provides little comfort during these challenging times. She feels compelled to share every scary hospital story she can think of – tales of accidental deaths, unnecessary surgeries, and the multitude of ways people meet their end.

And then there's Cousin Latrice, who somehow always manages to find a vending machine on her way up and shows up with about ten bags of chips, seven packages of cookies, some peanuts and two sodas, like she's at a movie theatre.

As we sat in a hospital room surrounding my dad, my thoughts turned to the hospital staff. They must have an iron will (or really good poker faces) to not laugh at the sitcom playing out in front of them. I mean, how do you keep a straight face when Uncle Baby Brother (yes, that's his nickname) starts flirting with Nurse Jackie, telling her how much she looks like his ex-girlfriend from high school, the one who got away, which is code for, the one he did wrong and she dumped him.

Are you kidding me?

No I'm not. Uncle Baby Brother was the light-skinned, green-eyed, football-playing, playboy in his school. In 2023 he's still light-skinned but his eyes are covered in cataracts, and he weighs about 350 pounds and walks with a cane and an oxygen tank. But you can't tell him he's not fine and the ladies don't still want him. And we don't have the heart to tell him that Nurse Jackie is just being nice. We watch him shoot his shot four times before he gets a clue. But Uncle Baby Brother won't be defeated. The minute Nurse Jackie leaves the room, he tells us, "She wants me. I'll drop by the desk and get her number on my way out."

I can't help but wonder if Nurse Jackie had to excuse herself to go laugh in the break room after Uncle Baby Brother's poor attempts at a love connection. It must've been like watching a live comedy show, only this time the comedian was completely oblivious of his performance. And let's not forget about poor Curtis, who probably thought his lengthy prayers were saving everyone's soul, oblivious to the fact that we were all silently praying for his prayer to end. It's funny how we all suddenly became religious in that moment, united by a common prayer: "God, please make him stop." And then there's Uncle Bernie, playing hospital cafeteria worker-turned-medical expert like it's no big deal. It's a good thing he retired before WebMD became a thing, or else we'd never hear the end of his medical advice. And let's not forget Felicia, our resident horror storyteller, who somehow manages to keep a straight face while we all try not to panic at her tales of medical mishaps. As for Latrice, I'm not sure whether to applaud her for finding the silver lining in a bag of chips or to question her priorities. One thing's for sure, though: there's never a dull moment when you're part of a black family dealing with a loss.

And this is only the beginning!

Chapter 2

A TURN FOR THE WORSE

When black families are informed that a loved one has taken a turn for the worse or there is nothing else that can be done, people start pouring in like they're attending the hottest concert in the city, not a hospital room. I don't know where they come from, but they're all there. Cousins you haven't seen in years, aunts and uncles that live on the other side of the state, and family friends from far and wide.

It's like someone sent out an emergency text, like one of those Amber Alerts or Tuesday afternoon broadcast signals. It doesn't make sense how quickly everyone shows up. And it's always the same thing: "I just came from work". "I was on my way to run errands and I pass right by here", or my personal favorite, "God told me I needed to come." Really? Did he also tell you to bring a change of clothes and your overnight bag?

But it doesn't matter how they got there, what matters is that they're there. And the hospital room suddenly becomes a lively gathering, complete with snacks and stories and laughter (as long as Cousin Curtis isn't leading the prayer). It's like a family reunion, only without all the planning and drama. And at this family reunion is Eugenia. Eugenia is what we call the professional mourner of the family. Think Wanda from the 70s sitcom, Good Times. She's always ready to drop some tears and a few moans and groans to really set the mood. You know she's around when you hear someone say "Oh, Eugenia's here." And sure enough, there she is, with her loud wailing and dramatic displays of grief.

Then there's Aunt Patty who is always on high alert. The minute anyone gets sick enough to go into the hospital, Aunt Patty is there, ready to go. I imagine my Aunt Patty was in the room waiting for President Obama to give the word to take down Saddam Hussain. The minute anyone calls Aunt Patty she is waiting and ready to disseminate the bad news. She answers on the first ring with, "Lord, Lord, Lord..." Before you can even share the news, she's ready to start making phone calls. Although she is torn up by the sad news, she is the family crier. She jumps on the phone and starts dialing everyone she can. Her goal is to be the one who tells everybody. She is on the phone snotting and crying to every aunt, uncle, cousin, neighbor, friend and third grade teacher.

Once word getts out, Aunt Patty is ready to grab the family and move forward with planning a funeral in record time. By the time the family returns from the hospital, Aunt Patty is on her way with the box. What box you ask?

The box with every single obituary of every person who ever died in the family, include Duke, the family dog. (not kidding)

The day of passing, which should rightfully be quiet and solemn, somehow turns into a crazy circus of emotions, stories, and family dynamics. And this is just the beginning. Buckle up, folks, because it's going to be a wild ride.

Chapter 3

FAMILY POUNCES ON THE HOUSE

Your beloved family member has passed away. You have said your final goodbyes and you leave the hospital to head home.

By the time you get home, there are twenty to thirty people waiting in their cars in front of your house. They are ready to console you.

For about thirty minutes, there are tears. Everyone is crying and it is so comforting.

Then it takes a turn.

The Wedding Photos Came Out!

You are not going to believe this but it's true. About one hour into the solemn time, Cousin Charlotte comes in with two large photo albums. She wants everyone to see the pictures from her daughter's wedding. They came just yesterday. Now we were all at the wedding, but she thinks now is the right time to go through these two massive photo albums and tell us in detail what happened that day. Did I mention we were all there?

So, while we are shocked with grief, she sits on the floor in the middle of the living room and starts describing the pictures, passing around these photo albums.

And not to be outdone, her sister Cathy, pulls out her phone with pictures from her 40th birthday party, which was this past weekend. And yes, most of us were there too.

Then, just when you thought the photo session was winding down, in barges Uncle Earl. Uncle Earl never owned a smartphone, and he always bragged about his reliable old flip phone. But all of a sudden, he had a smartphone in his hand. He had the determined look of a kid with a new toy, insisting, "I've got pictures too, only they're in my email." Now, keep in mind, Uncle Earl couldn't even spell 'email'. But there he was, fingers jabbing at the screen as if he were trying to crack a safe. His brow furrowed with intense concentration. We all watched, half in anticipation, half in sheer amusement. After about ten minutes of us trying not to laugh, he finally admitted, "I don't know how to work this thing!" And that was it. The room erupted in laughter, even amidst our grief.

Four rapid doorbell rings tell us Aunt Patty has arrived and you know what that means?

It's time for the obituary!

Chapter 4

THE OBITUARY

Aunt Patty arrives and her agenda is serious. She calls the room to quiet attention and demands everyone gather around. The room comes to order, and Aunt Patty pulls out "the box". Inside this rather large but well-maintained box is filled with...OBITUARIES. Aunt Patty is the keeper of the obituaries. She has a collection of every obituary for every family member who has passed away. As she pulls out the stack of obituaries, she starts to read them in order from oldest to most recent. Every now and then there is an interruption or a question.

"Who's that again?"

"That's Eugenia's sister-in-law!"

"Oh, I remember her."

"Yeah me too, she always had the best pound cake at the family reunions."

And so it goes, as we all gather around and listen to Aunt Patty recount the lives and memories of those who have passed on. Aunt Patty will also tell us what went wrong in the past, what facts were left out in past obituaries and how we have to make sure we get the facts right.

Everyone gathers around the table, with Aunt Patty leading the charge, and guess what? It's time to say a quick prayer! Lord, help us!

After the slightly shorter prayer than the ones at the hospital, we go through the obituaries.Then the phones come out. Everyone has a picture of themselves with the deceased that they want to be included in the obituary. I'm talking about every shot you can ever think of. Some of the photographs were taken when he was about 20 years old. Did I mention my dad died at 87? Some of the pictures have people in them who have either passed away years ago or they have been booted out of the family due to a divorce, disagreement, or just plain old bad feelings. So, as we go through the pictures and stories, Aunt Patty starts writing the obituary. And I mean writing it on paper! No computers in sight. Just good old-fashioned pen and paper.

The funniest thing about this whole ordeal is the things that are standard in every obituary, at least every black obituary.

The "Standard" Black Obituary - A Recipe for Remembrance With A Dash Of Drama!

- Sunrise to Sunset - In plain English, the day they were born and the day they died.
- Born to the union of... Parent's name.
- Preceded him in death... The siblings who died first.
- Gave his life to Christ at an early age... More often than not, this means the person hasn't seen the inside of a church since they were a child.

Now, here's where it gets interesting. There will inevitably be some kind of friction because everybody sitting around that table wants their name mentioned in the obituary. Nope, not kidding. Relatives have nearly come to blows because Aunt Patty didn't write their names down. And even though everyone knows that Aunt Patty will be the one to write the final obituary, relatives still want their say about what should and shouldn't be mentioned. And there will be no untruths with Aunt Patty in charge. In one obituary writing session, Aunt Patty refused to add the title "wife" to a long-time girlfriend. The deceased had actually written out his own obituary, but Aunt Patty stood her ground, refusing to include any mention of the title "wife" in the obituary. In the end, Aunt Patty won. The poor woman, after living with him for over 20 years was called, "his special friend."

Back to the obituary writing.

Now that we've established the rules for writing the obituary (Aunt Patty is the law), and the first page is complete, let's move on to the second page. This one is where Aunt Patty adds in all the details and accomplishments of the deceased. And by "accomplishments", we mean anything that can be remotely connected to a success story, no matter how small or insignificant it may be.

There's always a section about their work history, education, and outstanding military service record (even though most of them were just drafted, dishonorably discharged and certainly never saw any combat).

Then comes the really important parts - their hobbies and interests. And let me tell you, this is where it gets really interesting. We've had obituaries that list "professional shopper" as a hobby, or "avid fisherman" even though they haven't gone fishing since they were 12 years old.You might even find some of their favorite foods."He loved his pot of mustard and turnips every Sunday with some hot water cornbread."The goal of the obituary is to make the person sound better than they actually were. Not always an easy task.

Somewhere around page 3 of the obituary, there is the order of service for the upcoming funeral service.This requires a lot of discussion.Who will do the prayer, who will sing the solos, who will deliver the eulogy. And of course, there is always some family drama that comes up during this process. Arguments over who should speak or sing, and sometimes even a disagreement over the order of service itself.Who gets to go first, who should sing last. You get the idea.

The other 3 or 4 pages are filled with pictures, quotes, bad poems and other crazy stuff.

Like the time cousin Berta decided to read an original poem aloud during the service. She titled it "In the Arms of the Reaper," and it was as dreadful as it sounds. It started out bad and just got worse, with lines like "In the chill of the grave, Uncle doth sleep," and "With the worms he now doth keep." The whole family was in stitches trying not to laugh out loud, and Berta, bless her heart, didn't understand why we were all "crying so much" at her beautiful poem.

The obituary session ends when Aunt Patty says it's finished. She has meticulously handwritten the entire 4-page obituary. She has checked the facts against every other obituary in the box to ensure there are no discrepancies.The obituary is now complete.

And we haven't even called the funeral home yet!

Chapter 5

THE CHICKEN COMES POURING IN

No black family funeral would be complete without "funeral chicken". What is funeral chicken you ask? It's the cheapest chicken you can find in the city you live in. This could be a 10-piece bucket from a chicken restaurant chain or 25 wings from the neighborhood fish and chicken spot. Now the funeral chicken comes from everybody and anybody. The neighbors, the church, the school, the job. Either way, you will have a lot of chicken at the house in the days leading up to the funeral because everyone who shows up with an offering of condolences, also brings a 10-piece bucket of chicken. The day after my father passed away my brother and I counted 12 rotisserie chickens (Walmart had a sale) and six pans of every chicken from every place you can think of, even a few freshly fried from the kitchens of friends and neighbors.

So soon enough, your refrigerator is filled with all of this chicken. And don't forget about the sides that are also being brought in with the chicken. Potato salad, macaroni and cheese, green beans, you name it. Then there's also the cakes. Favorite funeral cakes include the infamous sock-it-to-me cake and the always available, 7-up pound cake. This is just the start of the food. Every day up to the day of the funeral, there is food. Tons and tons of food. Black love is in giving food. We celebrate with food, and we also mourn with food. By the time the funeral day arrives, you never want to see another chicken. Not like there's a chicken left in the city anyway.

Food is not the only thing that shows up. Oh no! There are gifts and supplies. People show up with sympathy cards filled with small amounts of money. You might get an elaborate Mahogany Hallmark sympathy card that costs $7 and inside there is a $5 bill. Then comes the supplies that no one asked for, but they figure you need it, so they bring it anyway. Things like a mop and bucket, laundry detergent, lotion, dish soap etc. Before you know it, your kitchen is stocked with all the cleaning supplies you can think of!

New to this funeral experience was toilet paper. Four people brought huge boxes filled with toilet paper. Not the good Charmin brand, instead this toilet paper was from the Dollar Store.

By the end of that first day following the loss, your house is stocked from top to bottom and you have enough food to feed an army and enough cheap toilet paper for said army.

Chapter 6

THE OUT-OF-TOWN FAMILY NEEDS A PLACE TO STAY

The next morning, the out-of-town family starts calling. Yes, they offer their condolences, but they also are quick to tell the bereaved family that they are coming. They are coming and most of your relatives don't want to rent hotel rooms. They want to stay at your house with you. Under the guise of wanting to help, they want to stay at your house. And they need a ride from the airport.

That's when the chaos really begins. We had aunts and uncles and cousins from all over the country who needed to be picked up and housed somewhere. This could be another family member's house but usually it's the house of the bereaved family. And if you don't have enough bedrooms for everybody, well then you better start making some pallets on the floor, i.e. beds, quilts and blankets spread out on the floor. The troops are coming and there's no way you could possibly be ready for what comes next:

Speaking of troops, have you ever tried herding lost relatives at an airport? Because that is a spectacle you've got to see. It's like a scene straight out of a slapstick comedy. Let me paint the picture.

Relatives we haven't seen in years and others we didn't even know existed start flowing in from all corners of the country. They're coming in from Detroit, Atlanta, L.A, you name it. And it's our duty to pick them up from O'Hare airport, one of the busiest airports in the country.

We pile up in the biggest cars we've got, Aunt Patty and her daughter (Aunt Patty Jr.). She's got the arrivals schedule scribbled on several napkins. We're like a ragtag taxi service, only instead of fares, we're collecting aunts, uncles, and cousins. Each arrival is an event - an eruption of laughter, tears, and "you've grown so much!" comments. By the end of the day, our convoy of cars, packed to the roof with family members, makes its way back home, to enjoy the never-ending supply of funeral chicken.

In case you don't have a clear picture, what ensues next is a house full of people who are crying, cooking, and literally moving into in your house, while you are grieving. Not to mention the fact that the toilet is always clogged because of all of these people who have never seen a plunger before, or maybe it's that cheap toilet paper. There's also a variation between the relatives who wake up before the crack of dawn and the relatives that want to sleep in. Picture cots and air mattresses all over the house while you're trying to grieve and plan a funeral. It's mayhem, kind of like those Allstate mayhem commercials – disaster waiting to happen.

Chapter 7

WHEN YOU BECOME THE VACATION TOUR GUIDE

While we're talking about the out-of-town family, we could not leave out the family members who use the funeral as a vacation trip. You know the ones. They want to go out for dinner every night and they drag you along in an attempt to show you a good time, even though you are about to bury your father. You find yourself in the car driving these relatives around your city on a sight-seeing tour. Depending on your city, you may end up at the casino, the beach, the museum, or the local water park. You become their vacation tour guide, and they will not take no for an answer. After all, it's a free trip for them that includes a free place to stay in your home.

And there you are, in the midst of your grieving, suddenly wearing the hat of a tour guide, chauffeuring the merry band of out-of-town relatives from one local attraction to another. They are armed with cameras and fanny packs, eager to take in the sights and sounds of your city. And you? You're just trying to navigate through this maze of grief and loss, but somehow you find yourself at the forefront of this impromptu vacation.

You're standing there, outside a bustling casino or a crowded museum, feigning excitement about the giant slot machine or the dinosaur exhibit. All the while, you're wondering how you got here.

During the week leading up to the funeral, the pressure of it all may become just a little too much. This is my sweet way of saying I snapped! "We are not going anywhere else. I am not your tour guide. If you want to plan a trip to come back later in the year, we can talk about it. But today, we're sitting in the house, eating some chicken and looking at each other."

Trust me when I tell you, it felt good. It felt so good, and it got everybody off my back for the rest of the visit. I heard whispers, "Poor thing, she's grieving. We might need to keep an eye on her. She might need to get some professional help after this is over."

So, if you find yourself in a situation like this, you might be labeled as the one who needs psychiatric help, but the outburst will fire you from the job of tour guide.

Chapter 8

PEACHES AND HERB

At 57 years old, I have been to a fair amount of family funerals. Inevitably there is a reuniting of some old love. Think back to the 70s song lyrics, *Reunited and it feels so good.* Peaches and Herb. There's something about mourning that makes old lovers reminisce. What is it about death that makes people forget why they broke up or why they stopped speaking to each other? All of a sudden, the past is forgotten, and old couples are reunited and in love all over again.

It never fails, every funeral I attend there's always at least one couple that has reunited because of the deceased. These couples come out of the woodwork; sometimes it's old high school sweethearts or the old childhood friend who's now cozying up to your brother. They are suddenly holding hands and whispering sweet nothings to each other, as if they are just meeting for the first time. It's like watching a real-life romantic comedy unfold right before your eyes. What is it about mourning that brings people back together? Maybe it's the reminder that life is short, and love is worth fighting for. Or maybe, as they say, death truly does bring people closer together. Or maybe mourning makes some folks horny.

Nevertheless, the Peaches and Herb syndrome is bound to show up in every family. In my family it's always Uncle James and Aunt Beatrice. They were married in 1966 and broke up in 1969. But they were never divorce and Uncle James always has some new woman he's living with. The family loves Aunt Beatrice and she is always welcome to sit with the aunts and cousins. But Uncle James brings his latest lady love, but the whole time he only has eyes for Aunt Beatrice. He has always loved her and something about funerals makes him want to rekindle that old love. Aunt Beatrice loves Uncle James, but she also knows him and she's not having it. She does her best to be polite and stay a safe distance away. His new woman is jealous. They always are. And after a few hours she is cussing like a sailor.

We've been at this for so long, that we usually start taking bets pretty early on how long it will take the for new love to lose her mind and fly into a jealous rage. When my dad passed away, I won the bet with 48 minutes. It took exactly 48 minutes for the new girlfriend, Suzie, to lose all sense of composure and scream, "James, get the F★★K back over here!" We all got a good laugh, as my brother and niece both slipped me the $20, they owed me. I timed it perfectly.

When it comes to getting back together again with an old love, here's a cautionary tale. It never lasts. Uncle James will be back to his latest girlfriend within a week of the funeral. And Aunt Beatrice? She'll go right back to her life, until the next family funeral and another sad love song of love reunited.

Chapter 9

THE FUNERAL HOME

Now that the obituary is finished, relatives are starting to be picked up, it's time to make a call to the funeral home. But guess what? We don't just go to any funeral home. No no, we have to find a "black" funeral home because black funeral homes know how to make black people look like themselves. (More on that in a minute)

You arrive at the funeral home. This is a money-making machine. It's the biggest hustle around. The funeral business is booming. You're mourning, crazy full of all the chicken, there has been a fight, reunited love, and now it's time to pick out the casket. The funeral home director slides a book in front of you and tells you they do have a room with samples if you want to see them up close. The first pictures in the book are your basic caskets. The photos in the book look like they were taken with a polaroid camera. The pictures are kind of grainy and not very colorful, because that's part of the hustle. The more expensive the casket, the more vivid the pictures. Now these pictures were taken with a professional camera with the latest technology. By the time you get to the most expensive caskets, inevitably, someone from the funeral home is now telling you all of the "features" of the casket. It's like when you're buying a car. They throw in the power windows, heated seats and tinted windows for free. Only this isn't a car, it's a casket! Who cares if it's heated, is triple sealed to keep out water and insects. Yes... that's a thing. And did you know you can purchase a casket on Amazon? A family friend shoves her phone in my face to show me the casket they chose for their mom that was purchased on Amazon. I wonder if they got Prime shipping!

Flowers are next. Same book ideas as the caskets. The first few pages are very bad pictures of flowers. Turn a few pages and the pictures are beautiful and the prices are up there. There were flower arrangements for two thousand dollars.

Don't even get me started on the cost of printing the obituary that Aunt Patty has painstakingly written out. One hundred copies of a color obituary with all those family pictures costs around $1600. And they use the UPS Store around the corner. The markup is 100% or more.

And because you're sad and grieving, you end up paying for it all, spending more money than you needed to. And there is no 30-day money back guarantee. No trade-in value. You just spent thousands of dollars on a one-time event. Talk about buyer's remorse. If you feel like you spent too much, it seems like you didn't love your person because who wouldn't want to give their loved one a beautiful funeral. The funeral home counts on that guilt. And so, the cycle continues. And you will pay the bill in full before the funeral or there will be no funeral.

Oh wait, there's more!

After you've picked the casket and the flowers, you're not done yet. You can start looking at memorial keepsakes. These are usually little trinkets that you can give out at the funeral to remember the deceased. You've got your basic picture frames, memorial candles, and sympathy wind chimes. But then you've got these extravagant crystal angels or jewelry with the ashes of the loved one. Urns with your loved-one's picture. They even sell blankets with the deceased's face on them. Just in case you want to get cozy with your grief, I suppose.

Then there's the guestbook. You need a guestbook so you can remember who showed up and who didn't, right? Of course, you do! Would you like a simple, classic, black leather book? Or maybe something with a silky cover that matches the casket? Or hey, how about this one that's made out of elephant hide and recycled paper?

Oh, and don't forget the thank-you notes. You know those cards you have to send out to everyone who came, gave a gift, or just said they were sorry for your loss. They have a whole book full of those too. You can get simple ones, fancy ones, or even personalized ones with your loved one's name and face on them. Because nothing says thank you like a reminder of the person they are grieving.

I'm telling you; these funeral homes are not playing. They are there to sell and they have everything you can think of and some things you can't. It's like a one-stop grieving shop. So, brace yourself, because entering a funeral home is like walking into a mini mall for the deceased.

Side bar: I could go give a dissertation on the lack of sufficient burial insurance in the black culture, but I'll save that for another time. It's not uncommon to see a GoFundMe page for funerals, Facebook posts with fundraising requests, and even bake sales. And... I also won't talk about the insurance money counters. Every family has someone in the family that is counting the insurance money and trying to figure out their cut. But I digress.

Chapter 10

FUNERAL OUTFITS

In the next stage of the funeral home visit, there is a decision to be made regarding the attire. This includes selecting the outfit for the deceased and could also include the outfits for the grieving family. The deceased will most likely be dressed in a suit or lovely dress. They will need everything from undergarments to jewelry, hats, and a tie. The ladies can have flowers in their hair or even glasses if the deceased wore them. We all know the saying "dressing for success". Well, this is dressing for afterlife, I guess. But... there are no shoes. You can be buried in glasses and a tie but not shoes. And what woman wants to be buried in a Spanx. That little tidbit came courtesy of the funeral director. We laughed as she shared of a recent family whose grandmother passed away and made them promise to put on her girdle so she would look thin. Maybe it' me but I hope looking thin in heaven isn't a thing. I don't get it but ok.

When it comes to the family attire, it's not uncommon for someone under the age of 35 to try to convince the family to wear matching outfits. Somehow this is supposed to make you feel more united as a family and shows how much you loved the deceased. But let's be honest, it's really a fashion show at this point. Somebody is going to be wearing something that shouldn't have worn and, even if you decide on matching attire, someone is going to take it way too far. The competition for the best-dressed person at the funeral begins now.

Old family friend, Barbara shows up with the outfit she wore to her 40th birthday party last month, glitter shoes included. Tyrone shows up with his pants sagging down past his butt and he has a t-shirt with a huge picture of the deceased. The picture he chose for the t-shirt is one where the deceased was partying, probably holding up the middle finger on one hand, while clutching a bottle of Hennessy in the other.

And let's not forget Great Aunt, Lucy. Aunt Lucy holds the title of diva. Aunt Lucy is always dressed to the nines. Even at the most casual of family gatherings, Aunt Lucy is decked out in high heels and diamonds. As one funeral ended, family and friends hugged and expressed their love for each other. It was a beautiful moment. Aunt Lucy, wearing a church hat that costs more than my first car, is standing proudly near the end of one of the pews. Her daughter, caught up in the emotional moment reaches to hug her mom and Aunt Lucy stops her dead in her tracks with a stern, "Tina, you know I don't hug in my Sunday clothes." Now before you get mad at Aunt Lucy, I have mad respect for her. In fact, I have respect for every funeral diva in every family. Why? Because no matter the circumstance, the family diva resolutely upholds her boundaries, never allowing anyone to overstep or abuse them. Not even at a funeral. Go ahead Aunt Lucy. I'm proud of you!

Chapter 11

HE LOOKS LIKE HIMSELF

The day before the funeral service is typically the viewing. Someone in the immediate family has to arrive early at the funeral home to make sure the body is ready to be viewed. They have to view the body to check that the clothing is right, hair and makeup is right and basically make sure it's your loved one. It's like before we put your loved one on display, we need your approval.

This is some twisted stuff. Who wants to come check the work of the funeral home? And do you know what we say when we get there? You know what we report back to everyone before the funeral service? We say, "he looked just like himself." Who the heck else would he look like? This is code language for the funeral home made him look almost alive.

And then somebody else says, "He looks peaceful." Is that really a thing? What would it look like if it wasn't peaceful. There's my favorite, "She looks just like she's sleeping." Which I really think is code language for, something is a little messed up, and I'd bet $10, it's the hair. Something about the hair is always off. I don't know who's doing hair in the back room, but it's usually not quite right. If not the hair, then something about the clothing is off. I immediately flash to the Mike and Molly episode where the sister,Victoria, gets chastised for putting glitter down a dead grandma's cleavage.

At this point, even if granny has glitter down her cleavage or grandpa's hair looks like a bad toupee, there's not much you can do. Remember, there's no buyer's remorse when it comes to funerals, no satisfaction guaranteed or your money back.

The viewing is to ensure that your loved one doesn›t look like a stranger in the casket.You get to see them before everyone else does.You also don›t want to be surprised at the funeral the next day. I think that›s what the viewing is all about. We need to have a preview of the funeral, kind of like the coming attractions for a movie.

Of course, something crazy often happens at the viewing. Queue the cousin who is an evangelist from some religion nobody's ever heard of. She walks into the viewing and wants to pray a chant or sing some words nobody understands. Well, it's inevitable that she will get a little too excited during this prayer/chant and bump into the casket. Now the casket probably won't move, but it will definitely scare the crap out of the praying cousin, enough to make her sit her tail down somewhere. And then there's always that one person who has no clue what to do at a viewing and ends up cracking jokes and making everyone else laugh. We all know it's inappropriate, but sometimes laughter is the only way to cope with the overwhelming emotions.

The viewing can also be a time for reminiscing and sharing stories about the deceased. It can be a beautiful moment of honoring their memory. In the black family, it's usually the preview of that's to come tomorrow at the funeral service.

Queue organ music!

Chapter 12

THE FUNERAL SERVICE

The day of the funeral service finally arrives, and everyone is dressed up and ready to pay their respects. The church is filled with people who knew the deceased, may have met them once or twice, or may have never met them at all. As the family leads to procession, making their way down the aisle, viewing their loved one and finally taking their seats on the first few rows. Everyone else then has an opportunity to walk around and view the body and offer their condolences to the family. Like they haven't been calling and dropping off chicken all week. This is the absolute longest thirty to sixty minutes of life. The bereaved family is sitting there. They cry a little, shake hands a little, hug a little but then you're just stuck, waiting, trying not to look at the casket. After 30 or 60 minutes, the casket is closed, and it's time for the funeral service. For a traditional Black family, this is a homegoing service.

Wikipedia defines the homegoing service this way:

A homegoing (or home-going) service is an African American and Christian funeral tradition marking the going home of the deceased to the Lord or to Heaven. It is a celebration that has become a vibrant part of African American history and culture. As with other traditions, practices, customs and norms of the African American culture, this ritual for dealing with death was shaped by the African American experience.

What it really means is. "It's time to have church"!

If you've never been to a Black homegoing service, you are in for a real treat. This is a hallelujah good time. There's a choir singing, a preacher praying a prayer that could take us all into heaven at any moment, and a soloist who is poised and ready to make everybody shout. Remember the obituary planning sessions? This is why it's so important. A lot of details go into making a service worthy of the deceased, but also worthy of the family. Nothing worse than a bad funeral.

Everyone has a copy of the obituary, and they are checking for their name and picture. Oh, did we forget that part? Something about us black folks in this generation, we want to see our picture as proof that we loved him or her so much so that we made the obituary. It's almost like a status symbol. I personally know of some people who are ticked off that they were not mentioned in some obituary of a family member, or the picture they gave didn't make the cut.

But all in all, the homegoing service is a true celebration. The soloist and the organ player are poised and ready to ensure that everybody gets their shout on. In fact, the organist and soloist are the main attraction. A lot goes into who's going to sing and who's going to play. This is actually more important that the preacher delivering the eulogy. A bad singer could ruin everything!

The Funeral Playlist
Top 10 Funeral Songs Designed to Get Somebody Into Heaven:

1. "Soon and Very Soon" by Andraé Crouch
2. "Going Up Yonder" by Walter Hawkins
3. "I'll Fly Away" by Albert E. Brumley
4. "Precious Lord, Take My Hand" by Thomas A. Dorsey
5. "Yesterday" by Mary Mary
6. "Something About the Name Jesus" by Rance Allen
7. "I Won't Complain" by Reverend Paul Jones
8. "Never Would Have Made It" by Marvin Sapp
9. "Order My Steps" by GMWA Women of Worship
10. "Stand" by Donnie McClurkin

Go ahead and get your shout on.

Chapter 13

REMARKS... 2 MINUTES PLEASE

After the praying, singing and shouting there comes a time for remarks. I don't know why we do this because at every funeral, this is the part where things go left. This is the part you have no control over, and this is the funniest part of every funeral. You never know who's going to say what and this is where the best secrets come out. At a funeral on TikTok, the pastor who was supposed to be preaching the eulogy actually proposed to the widow during the remarks. I don't know what about this section of a funeral makes people lose their minds. The minister or mistress of ceremony (person in charge of reading the upcoming events on the program) will typically ask for two minutes of remarks but trust me it's never just two minutes. Somebody always has something strange to say, and it usually has nothing to do with the deceased. But that's what makes it so entertaining. It's a glimpse into the lives of those who knew the deceased and their relationships with them. And sometimes, it's just pure comedy. This is where the magic happens. No matter what the instructions are, no matter how many times you say please limit your remarks to 2 minutes, somebody will do something crazy. Phyllis may jump up and sing a solo that she made up right there at the funeral. And Phyllis can't sing. She thinks she can, but she can't. This is the time where someone wants to share an inappropriate story about the deceased or tell how they owe them money. It's a mess. But it's funny.

After about 30 minutes of 2-minute remarks the preacher finally stands at the pulpit and delivers a rousing eulogy. If the person was a faithful church member, basically a good person, the eulogy is about them very specifically. On the other hand, if the person was a hot mess, doing all kinds of crazy stuff, the preacher has some work to do. This is where good preaching skills come in. You hear stuff like, "Brother Johnson was Brother Johnson. He was who he was, and we don't expect him to be any different." The entire church nods and says, "Amen." The preacher will then say, "But God knows his heart." This is code for we hope he made it to heaven but I'm not sure.

One thing you can always tell at a funeral. Who treated the deceased the worst. The person who was not nice or did something bad that they never got to apologize for. How do you know this person? They are the person at the final viewing of the body, screaming, hollering and climbing in the casket screaming, "Take me, don't go..." Do they mean it? Heck no. They are just guilty and clowning.

Years ago, my cousin was screaming and carrying on at her brother's funeral and my granny said, quite loudly, "Get your ass up before you knock the darn casket over. Tell him you sorry at the cemetery." Did we roll with laughter? Yes, we sure did. And my cousin got her tail up and sat down.

Just when you think there's nothing left to laugh about, let me share the story of Aunt Angel. At a funeral, she was overcome with uncontrollable tears—or so we thought. As we gathered around to comfort her, offering tissues and words of solace, we soon realized that her tears were actually laughter. Why the laughter? Uncle Joe had a freshly done Jerry curl. Angel whispers in fits of laughter, "It's 2022. He sat under somebody's dryer with all those tiny rollers in his head." Needless to say, we all laughed.

Chapter 14

THE CEMETERY

Before we head to the cemetery, this is the perfect time to tell you about Cousin Shelly. Shelly is not really a cousin, but she's been a family friend for so long that we call her cousin. Although Shelly is not technically a cousin, her longstanding presence in our family has earned her the endearing title of cousin. In every black family, there are individuals who have been a part of our lives since childhood, or who have been lifelong friends of our parents. Their unwavering presence has been a constant support throughout our journey, to the extent that they are considered honorary members of our family. As an adult, I discovered that some individuals I had always considered as my aunts, uncles and cousins were actually not biologically related to me at all.

Now, back to Cousin Shelly. Throughout the entire service, she remains perfectly still, her face expressionless and her arms tightly crossed. Shelly appears quite uncomfortable. In fact, Cousin Shelly is hot. Even when the singer hits the note that brings everyone in the church to their feet, Shelly is unphased.

Want to know what was going on?

Well, Cousin Shelly was angry because she didn't get to ride in the limousine with the family on the way to the funeral. She's been there every day. She's bought food, helped pick out pictures for the obituary and everything. How dare they not give her a seat in the family car?

We didn't find out what was actually going on with Cousin Shelly until we were at the cemetery. Here's the conversation between Cousin Shelly and real Cousin Raymond:

Raymond: "Shelly, what's wrong? You've been looking like you're at a tax audit instead of a funeral."

Shelly: "Well, Ray, I should be riding in style in that limo. I've done more for this family than some of those folks who got a seat!"

Raymond: "Shelly, you do know it's a funeral, right? Not a ride to the Oscars?"

Shelly: "That's not the point, Raymond! It's about respect!"

Raymond: "Well, I love how you just turned a funeral service into a debate about seating arrangements. Did you want a front-row seat at the church too? Should we have asked the preacher to move so you can sit up in the pulpit?"

Shelly: "Watch it, Ray. Keep talking and we might be back here next week for your burial."

Raymond laughs, shaking his head at Shelly's disgruntlement over her lack of a limousine ride. And just like that, the tension dissipates, leaving a trail of laughter behind.

Chapter 15

THE FUNERAL IS OVER BUT PEOPLE DON'T GO HOME

The funeral is over the body has been buried. In some instances, balloons have been released, liquor may have been poured out (for the homies who have gone on before). Kidding, but not kidding. Now it's time for more chicken and more family. And if you're lucky, there will be another fight that Big Momma will break up. The plates are passed, the red cups come out, the liquor starts pouring and the music starts jamming. Yes, we had a funeral at a church. We had a homegoing service but now it's time to party. The cards come out for several rounds of spades in the kitchen and Cousin Skip unpacks his turntables and sets up in the corner. Electric slide, the cha cha slide and steppers take the floor. Eventually someone grabs the widow, and she takes a spin on the dance floor, laughing and showing the family who she was back in her day.

The funeral is over, the stress begins to fade. There's nothing but family and a good time. Funerals bring out the personalities of those we have lost and it helps us to remember what made them special. The music, the laughs, the food and all of those memories will stay with us forever. I think back on family funerals and remember how much laughter was shared in addition to the tears. Even though we start off sad and filled with grief. Even though our family does weird stuff and there might be a spat or five, it's still family and we have nothing but love for each other. Family is what makes all the grief just a little bit better.

Chapter 16

GOD HAS A SENSE OF HUMOR

They say you can't choose your family. I believe this is because God has a sense of humor. In every family, there is a crazy aunt, a playboy uncle, and a few people who drink too much or talk too loudly. These are the people that make funerals the craziest. They cuss, they fight, but at the end of the day, we forgive each other and move on. It's not easy to laugh when someone dies, especially in our Black community, where death can be painful and sometimes tragic. But humor is one way to cope with loss, and I believe it's important to remember that even in death, God has a sense of humor. He put the crazy cousins, the uncle who can't let go of his ex-wife, the cousin who can't sing in your family. He put them all in your family, so at the right time, during the times of sorrow ad mourning, you would have something to make you laugh.

So even when we're sad, let's remember that laughter is medicine. Laughter is one of the ways our loved one live on in us. It's how we keep family memories alive.

That's family!

That's love.

That's what funerals are all about.

So, the next time you go to a funeral, remember to look for reasons to laugh through your tears. The journey of life is a crazy one, and the things we do to get through it are pretty amazing.

So, laugh on!

Place bets on the stuff you know can only happen when your family gets together. Count chickens and plastic containers filled with potato salad. Step over the sleeping Raymond from Alabama, who has slept on your living room floor until noon for four days. Find a favorite cousin or sibling that gets you and look for reasons to laugh. Don't forget to write them down. This can be your next bestselling book.

I wrote this book with my family while we were grieving. We laughed as we sat around the table without Aunt Patty. And we wrote down all these crazy stories. While one day, we will all end up in that obituary box, and while there will be crazy relatives doing crazy stuff, we will have had something most people long for: the love of a beautiful Black family. No matter how crazy they are, there is love. Let's never forget that. Because the best memories are made when you laugh with your family and friends. So, here's to living life to the fullest and laughing our way through it!

Now, go out there and make some memories! You know what they say: When the going gets tough, the tough get laughing!

I hope this book brought you laughter and made you smile. Because on the way to a funeral, some funny stuff happens.

Be blessed, Andrea

ABOUT THE AUTHOR

Andrea Oden is the CEO of AIR Network, a life strategist, author, and of course, everyone's favorite (or maybe not so favorite) funeral critic. She's your go-to girl for all things funerals - from the fights that break out, the crazy amount of chicken to the inappropriate dance-offs by the casket, she's seen it all.

When she's not writing about funerals and causing a ruckus, Andrea is also a highly sought-after keynote speaker, and the first woman to be ordained a minister at New St. John Community Baptist Church in Chicago, Illinois. She's currently holding the only license issued to a female by the church, but she's got plans to change that. Her mission is to equip women to stand in their truth, power, and authenticity - both in boardrooms and in churches, while laughing throughout the journey.

Andrea currently lives in a Michigan suburb with her family, but Chicago will always be home for her. She is usually found laughing with her family, writing about funeral shenanigans, or trying to wake up Raymond, who's still sleeping on her living room floor. Her greatest hope is that through her stories, you find the courage to laugh, even in your darkest hours. Because life is worth laughing at.

ACKNOWLEDGMENTS

I'd like to extend a heartfelt thank you to everyone who has sat around the table with our family in the days and weeks following our loss. Thank you for sharing stories and memories with us while we tried to make sense of our loss. To my family, who shared in the laughter and the tears, your love and stories have been the lifeline in putting this book together. Special thanks to my mom, the impeccable Lou Oden, for her unwavering support and her own unique sense of humor that has carried us through the toughest of times. There were times where we would catch your eye and see the laughter as something crazy transpired.

To my circle of friends, who have been sounding boards, cheerleaders, and late-night confidantes, your encouragement has been invaluable. And finally, to every reader who picks up this book during their time of grief, I hope these pieces of our story bring a smile to your face, a laugh to your day, and a little comfort knowing that even in times of loss, there's room for joy. Hopefully, you'll find yourself laughing out loud as you relate to some of these stories.

Here's to laughter - it truly is the best medicine.

★★★★★

If you **recognized yourself**,
a family member or if you laughed even a little bit,
please leave a **5-star** review on **Amazon**!

In case you remember some funny funeral stories, I left you a little room to write them down. You might write your own book one day!

ON THE WAY TO THE FUNERAL, FUNNY THINGS HAPPEN

ON THE WAY TO THE FUNERAL, FUNNY THINGS HAPPEN

ON THE WAY TO THE FUNERAL, FUNNY THINGS HAPPEN

ON THE WAY TO THE FUNERAL, FUNNY THINGS HAPPEN

MORE BOOKS FROM ANDREA ODEN

The Road Without You:
A Journey Through Grief

Losing a parent or loved one can feel like navigating a dark, unfamiliar road without a map.

In the face of a devastating loss, navigating grief can feel like a journey through the darkest night without a guide. Andrea Oden, your compassionate friend and experienced life strategist, delivers "The Road Without You", as a beacon of hope for those grappling with the loss of a loved one.

This book seamlessly combines introspective writing prompts, heartfelt prayers, and inspiring scriptures, providing solace during one of life's most challenging moments. It's more than just a book, much more than a journal - it's a route to healing and transformation, a call to uncover joy in the midst of the pain.

AN EXERPT FROM THE ROAD WITHOUT YOU

The Road Without You: A Journey Through Grief

Welcome, dear one. This is a journey you never asked for, yet here you are. It is your safe space, a harbor in the storm where you can honor your grief and tend to your heart. Grief is not an enemy to be conquered but a testament to the love that you lived and lost. And while you may feel broken by this profound pain, please know you are not alone. Although it may feel like it, you're not. There are millions of people experiencing grief at this moment.

The week after we buried my father, I saw more funeral processions than ever before. Those life insurance commercials with parents and children flooded my tv. It seemed as if everywhere I turned somebody was dying. Had it always been there, or was it my imagination?

Death is a constant presence, yet we often remain oblivious to its existence until it unexpectedly crosses our path. It's like purchasing a new car; you suddenly notice the same make and model everywhere you turn.

Grief is like this too. When you're in it, the world around you takes on a different hue, and everything seems to whisper, "You are not alone." So, take heart, my friend. Recognize that your suffering is part of something much larger than yourself.

Losing a parent is like entering a new world, one that can feel strangely foreign and unfamiliar. It's like being lost in an area once familiar. Losing a parent is like driving down a road that you've always known but suddenly not recognizing the houses, businesses, and street names.

You're standing on the edge of the unknown, not knowing which way to turn or how it will all end.

Welcome to your "Griever's GPS." Let us embark on this journey together, reminding ourselves that even in our darkest hours, we are alive, capable, and, most importantly, worthy of love and joy.

Scripture:

"The Lord is close to the brokenhearted;
he saves those whose spirits are crushed."
(Psalm 34:18, NLT)

This verse reassures us that during the painful process of losing a parent, when our hearts are most vulnerable, and our spirits feel crushed, God is near. He understands our pain, comforts our broken hearts, and grants us the strength to endure.

A Prayer for Composure

Dear Merciful God,

My soul is in deep anguish, and my heart is broken into a million pieces. The pain of my loss feels unbearable, and words fail to articulate the depths of my despair. I cry out to You in my sorrow, trusting that You hear my plea.

Your Word declares that You are close to the brokenhearted, and You save those who are crushed in spirit (Psalm 34:18). So, in this moment of heart- break, I'm drawing near to You, Lord. I am laying my pain, my disillusionment, and my sorrow at Your feet. Let Your peace wash over me, calming the storm within.

Please help me to remember that suffering isn't a sign of Your absence but a reminder of Your tender mercy and love. You have promised that You will never leave us or forsake us, and I hold onto that promise now.

I humbly ask this in Your Holy name, Amen.

Let's Journal Today!

The loss of a parent is like the loss of a safe harbor, of a piece of your foundation. It may feel like losing a part of yourself, but remember, their love lives on within you, guiding and strengthening you in ways you may not yet realize.

What stands out most vividly in your memory about the day you lost your parent? What thoughts and emotions consumed you that day? What was the first thought you had?

....

....

....

....

....

....

....

....

....

....

....

....

....

....

....

....

....

Award-Winning
Catching Hell Trying to Love a Black Man

Black women seem to be "Catching Hell" trying to fall in love and stay in love with a black man. This book takes a good, hard look at the problems facing black women and highlights why every woman should take an honest look at herself before placing blame on the black man. Andrea's brutally honest and tough-love approach will challenge readers to look at past relationships through a "Coroner's Report" view. Women learn quickly to accept responsibility, establish dating standards, and put firm and unmovable guardrails in place.

Andrea hits hard with the question, "Are you who...the person you're looking for...is looking for?

Before attempting your next relationship with a black man, give this book a try. You might be surprised to discover a new and improved you who makes better choices in the love department. You might even find the love you've been looking for -- a love made in heaven!

An Excerpt From
Catching Hell Trying to Love a Black Man

Long before Beyonce's anthem raising the roof saluting, Single Ladies, Natalie Cole sang the single woman's anthem of truth. She tells women to be careful of breaking up with a man they might miss later on. She says it's the little things you'll miss about him...helping with the groceries, helping in the yard, painting, repairing, huh, paying the bills. Her heart breaks as she says, "...now all I have is memories and regrets..." She bursts into the hook of the anthem..."I'm catching hell. Living here alone..."

I've felt this feeling, and I'm sure most single women have. The reason I've stayed in several relationships is to avoid this feeling. However, I've discovered that the hell of being alone is not nearly as bad as the hell of being in the wrong relationship – a bad relationship. And trust me, the relationship is bad if you are not happy.

Contrary to popular belief, there are some good men in the world. There are even some good, single, black men in the world. To get one, women have to do seven things.

1. Figure out what went wrong in the past
2. Discover who you are
3. Determine what the heck you really want
4. Learn to let a man be a man
5. Honor your true self
6. Patiently wait while enjoying your life
7. Let him love you when he comes your way

These seven steps have put me on the path to success concerning getting and holding on to the man of my dreams.

The scripture says in Proverbs 18:24, He who finds a wife, finds what is good and receives favor from the LORD (NIV). I'm a good thing, and I am woman enough to bring the right man favor!!!! What about you?

Are you a good thing?

Ladies, you can't be good if you're broken. You can't be good if you're bitter. You can't be good if you're still hurting and angry about the last man. And… you can't expect a man to fix you.

Love's Coroner's Report: Go Beneath the Surface and Find The Real Reason the Relationship Failed

Looking for closure after a breakup? Love's Coroner's Report can help. Guided journal prompts will help you uncover the real reasons your relationship failed, so you can learn from your mistakes and move on. With this report in hand, you'll be able to avoid unhealthy relationships in the future and finally gain some peace of mind.

Don't just accept that things didn't work out - find out why and learn from it. Love's Coroner's Report can help you do just that. So, grab your lab coat and get started!

An Excerpt from Love's Coroner's Report

You've just gone through a breakup. It doesn't matter how long the relationship was, it's still painful to go through a breakup. For most of us, there's that old nagging voice that loudly screams,

"You've failed again."

"Something must be wrong with you.""Why can't you keep a man?"

The relationship is dead. There's no pulse at all. It's gone. All the good times are gone, and the goodbye was painful. Now it's time for you to conduct an autopsy and review the coroner's report on what killed your relationship?

This book will help guide you in conducting an autopsy on your last relationship. It's important to know why your relationship died. Just like a true autopsy report, we will look beneath the surface to discover the true cause of death.

We will discover what killed the relationship, by understanding:

- Underlying Marks and Scars
- Evidence of Injury
- Forensic Details
- Findings
- True Cause of Death

So what is a coroner's report exactly? In an actual death it is a detailed report that summarizes the death and cause of death. In the actual death of a person, the coroner's report details the cause of death by looking on the surface and looking at internal injuries or external reasons that may have caused harm or death. In a relationship a coroner's report looks at what's beneath the relationship. In relationships we need to look beneath the surface and look at two individual people and what went wrong. The report should go beyond the surface and is an honest look at all death factors. Sometimes it takes a while to get to the root cause but the more you dig, the more you uncover. Sometimes, you might even have to call in another expert to help you uncover the cause of death. But please know an autopsy is a must to prevent dying from the same death over and over again. Many times, we keep entering into the same types of relationships and watching them die because we never clearly understand why a relationship ended

You are the coroner, but you can't blame the other person for everything. Take an honest look at yourself and how you contributed. Sometimes we simply made the wrong choice. Sometimes we stayed too long or weren't true to ourselves. We may have settled for something we didn't want. Let's look at your last relationship. Include as many details as you can. Be objective, as if you are the relationship coroner looking beneath the surface for the cause of death. Ready?

Let's go!

**The Breakup Journal:
Healing Love's Heartbreak One Word at a Time**

A breakup can be devastating.

No matter who ended the relationship, you're left with questions. Am I good enough? Will I ever find love? This guided journal is designed to help you take a loving look inside yourself.

With guided prompts, you'll be able to reflect on the root causes and love patterns that have previously defined your relationships.

Take 15 days and learn to love yourself. Learn to love yourself so wholly; every man watching will stand up and take notice and want to love you too.

Grab your copy today. Your future husband will thank you!

All Book by Andrea Oden Are Available Now on Amazon

Stay Connected with Andrea Oden
www.andreaoden.com
@theandreaoden on all social media platforms

Made in the USA
Monee, IL
03 November 2023

45715957R00044